What Do I Say?

TALKING AND PRAYING WITH SOMEONE WHO IS DYING

Margrit Anna Banta

Franciscan
MEDIA
Cincinnati, Ohio

Scripture passages have been taken from *New Revised Standard Version Bible,* copyright ©1989 by the Division of Christian Education of the National Council of the Churches of Christ in the U.S.A., and used by permission. All rights reserved.

Cover design by Mary Ann Smith
Cover image © Tetra Images | Jamie Grill
Book design by Mark Sullivan

LIBRARY OF CONGRESS CATALOGING-IN-PUBLICATION DATA
Banta, Margrit Anna.
What do I say? : talking and praying with someone who is dying / Margrit Banta.
pages cm
Includes bibliographical references.
ISBN 978-1-61636-804-3 (alk. paper)
1. Death—Religious aspects—Christianity. 2. Church work with the terminally ill. 3. Terminal care—Religious aspects—Christianity. I. Title.
BT825.B268 2014
259'.4175—dc23
2014019509

Copyright ©2014, by Margrit Banta. All rights reserved.
Published by Franciscan Media
28 W. Liberty St.
Cincinnati, OH 45202
www.FranciscanMedia.org

Printed in the United States of America.
Printed on acid-free paper.
15 16 17 18 5 4 3 2

Contents

Acknowledgments

I am grateful to my daughter, Dianne O'Donnell, R.N., who shared with me her considerable experiences with dying patients. She also has worked as a parish volunteer driver, taking terminal patients to the hospital for checkups and for chemotherapy appointments.

Thanks to Lorrie McMahon, a recent widow and good friend for sharing her experiences with me.

Thanks also to my grandson Wei Mo, an aspiring photographer, who took my picture with patience.

I am most thankful to my dear friend of over forty years, Reverend Joseph Slattery, for suggesting that I write this book and for his encouragement, support, and affirmation.

Introduction

Sharing the final journey of someone who is dying is one of the most difficult things we are called to do. But it can potentially be one of the most rewarding spiritual tasks as well. The main requirement is that we strive to be careful, caring, and attentive listeners. For the most part, we need not be able to provide any solutions or answers, but rather be honest, loving, and impartial listeners.

This is not an easy role. We seem to be more comfortable giving advice and trying to change things for the better. However, terminal patients who have accepted the finality of the situation often look for someone with whom they can share this profound and final experience of life.

Patients might share with you their deepest concerns, successes, failures, and life experiences. Simply by listening, you may be able to validate the experiences of a lifetime and in doing so offer comfort to them on the journey.

Your approach to this task will take different shapes depending on how close you are to the person who is dying, and whether you are a friend, a family member, an acquaintance, or a professional caregiver. The situation will also vary according to the age of the person dying, whether it's a sudden injury or a lingering illness, and many other factors. Throughout the process, though, the need to listen and be attentive to the other person's needs will be a constant.

I have written this book from the perspective of a pastoral minister who has cared for terminally ill and dying patients, as well as for their families and friends. I do not have any medical or scientific training in this area, so any thoughts and suggestions in this book come only from my own experience as a pastoral caregiver.

My mother was diagnosed with colon cancer when she was in her late forties. She had an operation and several bouts of radiation, which caused painful internal burns. Her suffering went on for about two years, and several times she attempted to talk to us about her situation.

My older sister and I were in our teens at the time, and my younger sister was just nine years old. Because of our ages, my father decided it was better for her and for us if we did not talk about her prognosis; we were not even to use the word *cancer* in her presence.

Now I realize it must have caused a great strain and hurt in my mother's life to not have been able to talk to her family about her illness. I pray that she found someone whom she could talk with at that time. I also pray that she has forgiven us for our silence.

When my mother was nearing the end of her life, she was admitted to the hospital with another bowel obstruction and my father, sisters, and I were taking turns being with her. One day, when it was my turn to be with her, I noticed she was very pale and weak but fairly alert. She recognized me, was able to speak, and asked for something to drink.

It was the time of year when my mother was usually canning fruits and vegetables, and I remember asking her for a recipe for canning gooseberries. She gave me the information I needed, and after that we talked about some everyday problems I was having. After a while, it was time for me to leave. We said good-bye, then I kissed her and left.

When I reached my home, I was informed that the hospital had called; she had died just five minutes after I left. I was stunned. I had no idea she was so close to dying. In retrospect, I think that she did not wish to upset me by telling me she was dying, knowing that as a family we were avoiding the subject.

It was years later that I realized the precious gift my mother had given to me on her final day on earth. She gave me an understanding of and sensitivity toward seriously ill people, which has prompted me to minister to the sick and dying throughout much of my adult life. Thanks, dear Mother!

Pope Francis recently said that we should not be afraid to love or to be tender in our work with others. Let this be our guide in the very important and sensitive task of caring for someone who is dying.

May the Lord bless you as you accompany another on this final journey.

TALKING WITH THE TERMINALLY ILL AND DYING

Jesus told his disciples, "If any want to become my followers, let them deny themselves and take up their cross and follow me." (Matthew 16:24)

Seriously ill people seem to know when death is near and they are often much more comfortable with that knowledge than most of the people around them. Even children who are terminally ill seem to have this knowledge. Some patients will set themselves a particular day, such as a holiday or anniversary, and seem to be able to survive until then. My niece wanted to live until her daughter's eighteenth birthday, and indeed, she died on the morning of that day. Another friend did not want to go into a nursing home, following a brief hospital stay. She died the night before she was to be admitted to the nursing home.

Although the patient may have accepted his approaching death, family members may not be ready to let the person go. That is why it is often easier for a friend, a pastoral minister, or a hospital worker to listen to the concerns of those who are dying.

Having someone to talk with can be a tremendous relief for most patients. Some test a number of different people before finding someone who can help them. One man said to me, "I don't know why all my children are coming to see me, because I haven't seen them in a while. I guess they think that I'm dying." Another person who had been diagnosed with a terminal disease gave me a book to read about someone who was dying of cancer. He had given the same book to two other people, who simply gave it back to him with a remark that was noncommittal. When I asked him if he identified with the person in the book, he immediately started to tell me about his illness.

If you think someone may want to talk to you about a terminal condition, listen carefully to what the person says about the state of his or her health. These remarks are often made suddenly and unexpectedly. For instance, something like "This is the last time I will be in the hospital," or, "I am coming toward the end," or, "The doctor tells me there is no hope," may all be openings for a further conversation about death and dying.

Such statements can take us by surprise, and we are at a loss how to respond. Yet sick people often make these remarks as they try to find someone they can talk to honestly and openly. Very often the person they choose is not a family member, because they may sense that their families are not ready to face the situation.

We know that our response is important, yet it is difficult to find the right words. Our first thought may be to deny the sad news and say something positive, thinking it will cheer the person. If we take that route, however, the sick person will know that he or she cannot talk to us openly and honestly about something that profoundly concerns them.

If you are able to walk with someone who is dying, you will become closer to that person than you ever thought possible. When someone feels comfortable talking with us, the most important thing we can do is listen. Attentive listening means nodding now and then, making eye contact, and acknowledging what you have heard. Remember that a lull in the conversation is not an invitation to break in and tell your own story or give an example of your own experience. It takes patience to listen and wait for the person to find the words to express what she is feeling, to say what is on her mind. Your presence, empathy, and attention are a priceless gift to the ill person.

Keep the conversation on the subject the sick person wants to pursue. Some responses to a difficult question might be, "Would you like to talk about it?" or, "What makes you think you are here for the last time?" or just, "Tell me about it." Let the person know you are willing to really hear what he has on his mind.

Most of the time, the person is not looking for answers, but just looking for someone to talk to about the many concerns involved in end-of-life matters. Keep the conversation going for as long as the patient wants to talk. Don't try to press for more than someone is willing to give, but be open the next time you visit. The patient may take up the conversation again, knowing that you are someone who is willing to listen.

It is important that you make time to visit as regularly as possible, and be ready to listen and to respond sincerely to any remarks or requests. Try to be available when the patient is not being cared for by hospital staff or another caretaker—for example, after mealtimes or in the evening before the patient goes to sleep. This can provide an opportunity for the person to talk or simply share your company in silence.

If the patient is unable to hear or to speak, touch may be your best way of communicating your love and concern. Be aware of body language, facial expressions, fidgeting: Does the person seem distressed or agitated, or is there a quietness, a peacefulness about his or her demeanor?

If the person seems restless, speak in a soft voice and ask if there is something she needs. Sometimes a person who cannot speak is able to squeeze your hand or blink when you ask a question. In this way you can find out if she is in pain or has any other needs. You might also want to offer a prayer. Often, someone is simply looking for assurance that they matter, that they are not alone.

Chapter Two

HONESTY AND DENIAL

Peace I leave with you; my peace I give to you.... Do not let your hearts be troubled, and do not let them be afraid. (John 14:27)

It takes trust, real honesty, and true compassion to sustain a relationship with a dying person. Some patients will repeatedly test you to see if you can continue on this journey. Patients seem to be extremely sensitive toward others and do not want to upset them. It's not easy to be honest at times like this. Our society has conditioned us to be polite and avoid causing pain. However, the terminally ill person looks for honesty.

Even though physical healing may no longer be possible, the patient may seek inner healing, being reconciled to his or her situation. This kind of healing takes attentive listening and compassionate awareness of what the patient is trying to convey. In this way we can bring healing to each other: the one who is dying and we who are present to the person through this process.

One man who was dying of cancer told me he would continue to do ministry as long as he "looked good." One day he stopped by to see me and asked, "How do I look?" He was very pale, his lips were nearly without color, and he had dark circles under his eyes. Knowing why he was asking me, I said, "You do not look good." He responded, "That's right!"

The man's response let me know he appreciated my honesty. In his eyes, I had passed a critical test. After that he discontinued his ministry, and he continued to confide in me until he died. When his time came, he was ready and at peace, and I felt privileged to have been able to share his last weeks with him. This man was not a relative, yet I had a very close bond with him.

If someone asks you to clarify his condition, you may want to ask him first: How much do you want to know? From the answer, you will be able to ascertain if he is ready for the complete truth of his condition or if he is looking for hope. He may just want clarification of a diagnosis.

One patient I went to see in a veterans' hospital had a visit from his doctor while I was there. The young doctor asked that I stay, then informed the patient very matter-of-factly that his condition was terminal and that he had just a few days to live. After the doctor left, the patient asked me what the doctor had said, because when he heard the word *terminal* he did not comprehend anything else. Over time, as we talked about his condition, he slowly started to accept the prognosis.

Denial

Denial is a natural response to devastating, life-altering news. It is one of the stages of death and dying identified by Elisabeth Kübler-Ross. If you are accompanying someone on this journey toward death, you will most likely encounter it at one time or another. What can we do in cases such as this? Our honesty and openness will go a long way toward helping them find peace during this very important time in their lives. Often it is best to go along with what the person is saying. We might more strongly affirm those statements that indicate an approaching acceptance of the situation. Contradictions at a time like this may not be helpful and can increase a person's agitation.

Sometimes a sick person is unable to accept his prognosis, even after a considerable period of time. He may seek a second opinion and try various protocols, alternate medical treatments, and anything that offers a promise of returned health. He may question the results of a test, wondering if there was a mix-up.

At times like this, someone might need to move the conversation in the direction of accepting the prognosis. A family member or close friend might find this difficult because of his or her own emotional involvement. Perhaps a hospice worker or pastoral care minister can be asked to talk to the patient. This is a difficult task, but it could bring a measure of peace to the person and his family. More important, it may help the person to see that they are doing things that could harm them further.

Patients who have had to cope with adversity throughout their lives are often better able to accept their diagnosis and adjust to it. Most patients will eventually come to face the reality of their approaching death and slowly give up the hope of recovery. This process can be much more gradual for close family members who continue to hang on to the hope of recovery.

Often the family members of the dying person are unable to accept the bad news. Especially if the illness or injury is sudden, shock can prevent those around the dying person from accepting the finality of the situation.

A young man was dying of encephalitis. Even though he was on a respirator and no longer conscious, he looked robust, tanned, and fit. He had been a regular cyclist and had enjoyed good health. One day, his mother was sitting next to his hospital bed looking very stoic. As the next of kin, she had been asked to agree to the disconnection of the respirator. Because she was in a state of shock, she was totally unable to function, much less make the required decision. Eventually, the family was able to convince her to disconnect the respirator.

At times the person who is dying is at a different stage of acceptance than his family and friends. I recall a man whose cancer had come back after a long remission. He was a very spiritual man and had made his peace with the finality of his prognosis. Yet when I spoke to his wife at his bedside, she was full of plans for what she and her husband would do after his recovery. They were going to redesign the yard, add a fountain, and expand the porch. Then they were going on the cruise they had always wanted to take. When I pointed out to her that her husband was getting weaker each time I saw him and less able to care for himself, that his prognosis was not good, she got angry with me. It was difficult for her to provide him with the support and acceptance he needed in his final days.

The process of coming through denial to acceptance can often take a long time. We need to remind ourselves and those to whom we minister that except in the most tragic situations when death happens very quickly, that time is often available to us if we are willing to be patient with ourselves and one another.

A young woman came to see me one day, very upset. Her mother had been battling cancer for some time. After several courses of chemotherapy, she had lost all her hair and a great deal of weight. Recently, the cancer had returned and the doctor had told the mother that she could not tolerate any more treatments.

When the daughter next visited her mother, she was informed about the latest prognosis. Her mother wanted to talk about this, but the daughter was unable to respond and left the hospital after a short time, very upset. When she came to see me, she was very unhappy because she felt that she had let her mother down and could not find a way to undo this.

I told her that her mother was probably waiting for her and that one can always return to the subject the sick person had initiated. If you visit someone and miss an appropriate response or find yourself unable to talk about a painful subject at the time, you can always pick up the conversation at your next visit, but don't wait too long.

She then went back to the hospital and said to her mother, "The last time I saw you, you wanted to talk to me about ending chemotherapy. I am ready to talk about it now."

The mother told her daughter about her fears and her worries for those she would leave behind. She said that she did not want to die in the hospital.

The daughter brought her mother home and made arrangements with her mother's doctors to ensure she had pain medicine on demand and was comfortable. During this time, mother and daughter cried together, hugged, held hands, and continued to support each other. After a few weeks, the mother died at home, in her own bed and surrounded by her loved ones, as she had wished.

When I saw the daughter following her mother's funeral, she told me that the last weeks with her mother were the most special of her life. She had gotten to know her mother better than she ever thought she would. These last weeks were a gift for both her and her mother, and the daughter was now at peace with herself and with her mother's death.

Chapter Three

UNRESOLVED ISSUES

Standing near the cross of Jesus were his mother, and his mother's sister, Mary the wife of Clopas, and Mary Magdalene. When Jesus saw his mother and the disciple whom he loved standing beside her, he said to his mother, "Woman, here is your son." (John 19:25–26)

*D*ying persons sometimes fight to stay alive because they have issues that need to be resolved. Unfinished business may weigh heavily on those who know that their time on earth is limited. Some of these unresolved issues can seem trivial to those around the dying person; other issues can be difficult and challenging.

When my mother was dying, she asked me to go to her closet and take out a particular dress. I asked her if she wanted to wear it that day, but she replied that this was the garment she wished to wear in her casket.

Although it made me sad to think about that, I was able to do that for her when the time came. It had been on her mind, and now it was resolved.

Some time ago, I visited a woman who was in a nursing home. She told me that a desk she had promised to a mutual friend had been taken by a cousin to whom the woman had given power of attorney. She asked me to let the friend know that she was sorry about what had happened to the desk, and I assured her that I would. Resolving this issue brought her peace, and just two days later I received a phone call telling me that she had died.

A teen or young adult who is suddenly faced with a terminal illness will have other issues. He or she will mourn many expectations and dreams that will not be fulfilled—perhaps a family of his own, travel, education, a career, accomplishments in a sport, art, or music; he or she may want to talk about each of these losses.

For a parent, leaving a spouse and children behind can add to the pain of dying. Who will take care of the children after he or she is gone? Are the financial needs of the family covered? Who will see to it that the children continue to be raised in the faith?

A few years ago, a young father who had recently been widowed came to see me. He told me that he had inoperable liver cancer, and the prognosis was that he had about three months to live.

His daughter was preparing to receive her First Communion, but the ceremony would not be held for another five months. It was very important to him that his daughter receive First Communion; he had promised his wife, who had died a few months before, that he would see to it.

I promised the man that I would work with his daughter's religious education teacher to make sure she received the Eucharist. With this, he was able to die in peace, knowing that his promise to his wife was being honored. On the day of the girl's First Communion, her catechist and I arranged a little party for her afterward.

At a time like this, the family should be encouraged to seek help through other family members, church resources, social services, and other opportunities that may present themselves. There is so much to be considered in this emotionally charged time that no one should have to rely on his or her own resources alone. Support the family in their concerns, and help them with their needs as you can.

Unfulfilled expectations, unhealed relationships, or other unfinished business can cause emotional pain that is often eased by supportive listening. You may feel helpless at times, thinking you should offer some concrete advice, but we often don't have the knowledge or expertise to help resolve these issues. Know, however, that you are helping the person find some inner peace by simply being there, with your companionship and loving presence.

Some of the most difficult situations can be family rifts due to prior hurts, insults, abuse, or neglect. You might offer to contact the family member or someone else in the family who may be able to offer help with resolving the situation—or at least talking it through. If the unresolved issue involves forgiveness, ask if the person would like to see a priest or minister or a pastoral counselor.

Sometimes the hardest person to forgive is oneself. The dying person may need to forgive him- or herself for a failure of some kind, or a situation in which they caused hurt to others. It might be helpful for the person to talk this out, looking at the choices they made and why they made them.

In instances where forgiveness is an issue, the story of the Prodigal Son (Luke 15:11–32) can be a comfort. This account of how a father welcomed back his son with great joy after they had been estranged is one of the most loved and recounted stories in all of Scripture. If you share this story, remind them that no matter what has happened or how others have responded, God is always waiting with mercy and forgiveness.

There are a number of other ways you can help a patient deal with unresolved issues. The person may wish to leave a letter for a loved one. If he or she is unable to write, you could offer to do that for him or her. Another option is to record the person as they speak and share that with whomever the person directs.

If the dying person doesn't have a will, ask if they want you to call an attorney. In some states, a hand-written will is legal as long as it is witnessed by two people who are not beneficiaries. The best thing to do is contact a lawyer about what can be done for the person.

By helping the dying person with unresolved issues, you will be able to help them find rest and inner peace. Being able to express their feelings and their concerns about unresolved issues can bring about emotional healing, as well as a sense of closure. This can lead to solace and tranquility in their final days.

Chapter Four

THE IMPORTANCE OF TOUCH

He stretched out his hand and touched
him, saying, "I do choose. Be made clean!"
Immediately his leprosy was cleansed.
(Matthew 8:3)

$\mathcal{R}$esearch has shown that a mother's loving touch
is essential for a newborn's development. According
to the University of Miami Touch Research Institute,
newborns who are frequently touched have supe-
rior mental and motor skill development. The same
research shows that seniors in our society receive the
least amount of touch of any age group. Yet the find-
ings are clear: among other benefits, touch can lessen
pain, slow the heart rate, and help us to relax. Touch
is reassuring, healing, nurturing, and helps us feel
connected to one another.[1]

Touching is an ancient way of healing, still prac-
ticed successfully in some other cultures. In Germany,

for instance, doctors often prescribe massages to heal specific illnesses, and massage is covered by national health insurance there. (Recently, some insurance companies in the United States have approved costs connected with therapeutic massage as well.) Doctors routinely prescribe physical therapy after an illness or injury, as this aids in the healing process.

Touch can be an act of kindness when someone is dying. If you visit a sick person and find that you are at a loss for words, reach out and touch her hand. If you are comfortable with the person, you might want to rub her arm, or use some hand lotion on her hands. It will convey your care for her and can have a calming effect. It says to the person, "You are appreciated, you are cherished, you are connected, and you are not alone."

In our society, touch is something with which we are not always comfortable. We must respect the boundaries people have in regard to being touched. For some people, it can be an uncomfortable experience in general. For others, an illness or condition may make them sensitive to touch. In all cases, we must gauge the level of contact appropriate to the situation.

Every one of us has the ability to be a healing presence and provide spiritual companionship to someone who is dying. To touch gently is to give hope—not the false hope of a recovery where none may be possible, but the hope of a tangible presence of God in our lives.

I recall visiting an older man in a nursing home who was in the final stages of dying. He had never been married and had no relatives in the area, and there had been no visitors besides me in the months I came to see him. He had lived alone in a small cottage for many years, and I suspect he must have felt very alone and isolated, his need to be touched very strong.

On one occasion when I was visiting, the man was trying to tell me something, but I had difficulty understanding him. He was unable to speak in complete sentences and could barely utter a few words. After several attempts to hear him, it turned out that what he was trying to say was, "Hold me." I bent over his bed and put my arms around him, and he relaxed. When the position became uncomfortable for me and I wanted to withdraw, he became agitated, so I continued to hold him until he fell asleep.

One of my most vivid memories of a bedside experience occurred when a beloved mother was dying.

There was an adult daughter on either side of her bed, each one holding her hand and caressing her arms. She died very peacefully.

Chapter Five

REVIEWING LIFE

For the LORD is righteous;
he loves righteous deeds;
   the upright shall behold his face.
(Psalm 11:7)

$\mathcal{A}$s people begin to move into their later years, they often go over what has happened in their lives so far: the accomplishments, the disappointments, the successes, the choice of a partner or of an occupation. If they have children, they may reflect on the effort of raising them, their education, their life choices, and their present situation, and they may think about how they, as parents, contributed to their children's lives.

Often in midlife people come to the realization that some of their dreams have not been fulfilled or may never come to pass. Sometimes, it isn't until later on, perhaps after retirement or when a serious illness strikes, that a person takes the time to look closely at his life.

When a person is dying, the events of his or her life may come sharply into focus. The end of one's life can be a time for looking back in a positive way at what one has done with his or her life. Family traditions, vacations, friendships, special occasions, and the like, are evidence of a life well lived, and can give meaning and purpose at the end of one's days.

A person may want to leave a life story behind as a legacy to family and friends. Recalling not only the good times but also the difficulties can bring comfort as someone prepares to leave this life.

If the sick person is willing, you might want to have a conversation with them that could be videotaped or recorded. Family members can be invited to join in, if the sick person is comfortable with this. One of my daughters videotaped an older aunt as she spoke about the memories of her life, and hearing her voice became a source of comfort for the family after she died.

In talking about their lives, many people prefer to choose a person who is not close to them, someone they can be impersonal and relaxed with, and whom they can trust. Family members may be too close to the patient and still hoping for recovery when the patient has already accepted his situation and needs to move on.

My daughter, Dianne, told me the story of how, as a volunteer driver for her church, she would take a terminally ill patient to treatment once a week. Immediately upon entering her car, this man would start talking about unresolved family and personal issues. He knew he was not going to recover, and this was his way of finding some validity, purpose, and peace in his life, and to ascertain that he had made the best decisions he could at the time.

Talking about one's life can be a slow and lengthy process, and sometimes painful as the speaker remembers events that caused disappointment or pain. In voicing these issues, the person can often come to terms with the decisions that were made as well as with the circumstances of his life. It's a way of externalizing the events, successes, and tragedies that have shaped him.

A minister I knew wanted to talk about his decision to take a new assignment away from the congregation he was currently serving after being diagnosed with terminal cancer. He wanted to continue to minister until he no longer could, but he did not want the people of his former congregation, with whom he had become very close, to be distracted by his illness. He felt that he needed to be in a completely new place to be an effective minister in the time left to him.

Not everyone has the patience to listen to someone as they unburden themselves. What is required? You should be nonjudgmental and attentive, simply validating the experience of the speaker. You do not have to help to resolve any controversies or have solutions or suggestions for the patient. All that is required is that you listen and confirm what you hear while being attentive and compassionate.

If the patient would like to leave a special message for someone, you might offer to write down her words and see that they get delivered. If there is someone with whom the patient would like to talk, offer to dial the number and then give her privacy. The fact that you take the time to be available and listen to her concerns can give her a sense of being valued, respected, and cared for.

Chapter Six

DEALING WITH DOUBT

About three o'clock Jesus cried with a loud
voice, "Eli, Eli, lema sabachthani?" that is,
"My God, my God, why have you forsaken
me?" (Matthew 27:46)

When all of our defenses have been broken
down, when hope for a recovery has died, when we
have to accept the inevitability of death, it is normal
to question our belief in God, in the soul, in heaven.
A patient may ask questions such as "Is there really
a loving God? Why hasn't God heard my plea and
helped me to recover? Where will I go when I die?"

It may help to realize that even saints and holy people
have experienced periods of doubt about the existence
of God. St. John of the Cross, a sixteenth-century
mystic, spoke about "the dark night of the soul," when
an absence of God's presence is felt profoundly. St.
Thérèse of Lisieux called this experience "a night

of nothingness." As he was dying on the cross, Jesus himself cried out to God, his Father: "Why have you forsaken me?"

Closer to our own time, Mother Teresa of Calcutta experienced years of doubt even as she continued to do her remarkable work, tending to the poor in India. Here are the words of Mother Teresa, written during the time of her darkness:

> Lord, my God, who am I that You should forsake me? The child of Your love—and now become as the most hated one—the one You have thrown away as unwanted—unloved. I call, I cling, I want—and there is no One to answer—no One to Whom I can cling—no, No One.... Where is my faith?—Even deep down, right in, there is nothing but emptiness & darkness.—My God—how painful is this unknown pain.... I have no faith—I dare not utter the words & thoughts that crowd in my heart—& make me suffer untold agony. So many unanswered questions live within me—I am afraid to uncover them.... When I try to raise my thoughts to heaven—there is such

> convicting emptiness that those very thoughts
> return like sharp knives & hurt my very
> soul.... I am told God loves me—and yet the
> reality of darkness & coldness & emptiness is
> so great that nothing touches my soul.... Did
> I make the mistake in surrendering blindly to
> the call of the Sacred Heart?[2]

Mother Teresa had written these troubling thoughts to Fr. Joseph Neuner, who told her several things with regard to this darkness:

- that she should not feel responsible for it, and that there was no human remedy for it
- that feeling the presence of Jesus is not the only proof of his being there, and that her craving for God was a sure sign of his hidden presence in her life
- that the absence of God was a part of the spiritual side of her work

Fr. Neuner also told her that her suffering was nothing less than a sharing in Christ's Passion. She was encapsulating in her own life the moment on the cross when Jesus asked, "My God, my God, why have you forsaken me?" Her perseverance in the face of it was echoing his faith until the end on the cross—it was a grace, a share in his passion that would enhance the effectiveness of her calling.[3]

When a person of faith expresses deep doubts about God, perhaps the best thing you can do is pray with that person. Remind him of all the good things he was able to accomplish in life and the blessings that came to him throughout his life. Talk about his talents, the people he loved, and those who loved him, reminding him that these are reflections of God's love. Help the person make a list of these experiences and accomplishments, and pray in thanksgiving for each one.

Ask the person what would give him comfort— a Bible, a cross or a rosary, a visit from a priest or minister. Remind him also that you care about him and will continue to pray for him, even when he is no longer with you.

Perhaps we, as human beings, need to go through this feeling of being stripped bare, of facing our deepest doubts and fears, of leaving our ego behind, so that we may finally be totally receptive to giving up our lives to God, the source of all life. This passage from the Acts of the Apostles is a powerful refection of staying faithful during times of darkness and doubt. Share it with the person, and keep it close to your own heart.

You that are Israelites, listen to what I have to say: Jesus of Nazareth, a man attested to you by God with deeds of power, wonders, and signs that God did through him among you, as you yourselves know—this man, handed over to you according to the definite plan and foreknowledge of God, you crucified and killed by the hands of those outside the law. But God raised him up, having freed him from death, because it was impossible for him to be held in its power. For David says concerning him,

"I saw the Lord always before me,
for he is at my right hand so that I will not
be shaken;
therefore my heart was glad, and my tongue
rejoiced;
moreover my flesh will live in hope.
For you will not abandon my soul to Hades,

or let your Holy One experience
corruption.
You have made known to me the ways of
life;
you will make me full of gladness with
your presence." (2:22–28)

Chapter Seven

FINAL ARRANGEMENTS

The LORD is my shepherd, I shall not want.

He makes me lie down in green pastures;

he leads me beside still waters. (Psalm 23:1–2)

There are a number of issues that have to be addressed before a person dies, such as signing a DNR (Do Not Resuscitate) order, a living will, deciding who will have power of attorney if that becomes necessary, and other concerns. If you are a spouse or the closest family member, you may be in the best position to talk about these issues with your loved one. Sometimes, however, it may be too emotional for you to approach this topic, in which case you might seek out the help and advice of a social worker or health care professional.

Someone will need to determine the patient's wishes concerning the use of feeding tubes, respirators, or resuscitation; if the patient cannot communicate his wishes, someone will have to make these decisions for him. Health care workers may ask for a medical directive that gives some of this information, and they may also ask if someone has been granted a medical power of attorney. If these arrangements do not exist, the next of kin will be consulted on end-of-life matters.

When they are dying, most people would prefer to be at home or in a familiar, comfortable place, surrounded by their loved ones, pets, and the memories of a lifetime. Yet according to statistics, 70 percent of patients die in a hospital.[4]

If the sick person is a member of your family, can you provide a place in your home for her to spend her last days? If so, you will need help with this. Ask the medical staff or a social worker to refer you to hospice care. These organizations have nurses trained in end-of-life care and can help to arrange for necessary equipment, such as hospital beds, to be rented and delivered to your home.

Hospice services also operate in some hospitals and in homes for the elderly, such as nursing homes and assisted-living facilities. The goal of hospice is to make the end of one's life as comfortable and pain-free as possible. It can help a patient and his family live fully until the end. Hospice care can also connect you with chaplains and provide personal visits and advice for the caregiver.

Other decisions will have to be made concerning the funeral and the burial. It is helpful to know what the dying person wants, if he or she is able to talk about this. Some people are not interested in planning the funeral and may be distressed at the suggestion. On the other hand, when my niece was dying of cancer, she wanted to make all the arrangements for her funeral herself; she even selected her own funeral urn. After everything had been arranged, she died very peacefully.

Here are some issues you may want to address with someone before they die:

Does the person want to be buried or cremated?

Does he want to donate his body to science or be buried at sea?

Is there a certain place where he would like to be buried? Does he have a burial plot? Who has the information concerning the plot and the cemetery?

What kind of funeral service would she like? Is there a priest, deacon, or minister whom she would prefer to conduct the service?

Does she have any requests for readings or for music? Many churches have suggestions for both readings and appropriate music for a funeral Mass or service. If the patient is able, she may want to make some of these choices herself, with your help.

If he was a veteran, does he want military honors at his funeral? Contact the Veteran's Administration and ask the funeral home to make the required arrangements. The VA or another local veterans' office should be able to help determine what paper-work is needed and whether additional benefits are available.

Is there a will? If so, where is it kept? Who is her lawyer? Does she have a safe deposit box? Who has access to it? Where is the key?

Does she have life insurance? Who is the provider? Who is the beneficiary? Are the necessary documents available?

Concerning other assets, does he have any invest-ments or a broker? Where are all his bank accounts, checks, credit cards, insurance policies, and the like? Does someone have power of attorney to access these accounts?

Does the person receive regular payments that are deposited into the bank account, such as pensions, annuities, social security, and so on? These providers will have to be notified following the death. If he owns real estate or a vehicle, ask an attorney how to transfer these assets.

Are automatic payments made from her account? Where are the records kept? Make sure that someone who can be trusted has the log-ins and passwords for any online accounts.

Does the person have some personal items she would like to leave with specific people? This may be spelled out in the will, but if not, it would be good to have this in writing.

Would the person like to leave a note for someone? You could help with that if he is unable to write.

These are just some of the decisions that will have to be made, whether by the dying person or by the next of kin. The more questions answered ahead of time, the easier it is for all involved. The family can be more at peace in the days following the death of their loved one, knowing that they have followed his or her wishes.

APPROACHING THE ARMS OF ANGELS

The souls of the righteous are in the hands
   of God,
and no torment will ever touch them.
(Wisdom 3:1)

*I*n cases of terminal illness or advanced age, as the person gets closer to dying, the body will begin to shut down. Changes will occur over a period of weeks, or in some cases, just days. Each person is unique, and the length of time approaching death will vary, but some physical changes are common to most patients who do not die from a traumatic event.

These are the most common:

Weakness, energy loss, and fatigue. Less energy is available for the usual tasks of life, and there seems to be a loss of interest in what formerly was important. The patient may become depressed or impatient over this loss of energy. Caregivers and loved ones need to assure her that she is loved and that the tasks required of her are not burdensome. The patient may want to talk about her concerns and perceived failings, or about needing more help and having her personal needs taken care of. Assure her of your concern and the constancy of your care. Remind her of times in the past when she helped you or others and that it is now her turn to receive such help.

Less interest in family or others. For many patients, visitors are becoming less important, as it takes a certain amount of energy to entertain guests. There is a noticeable withdrawal from social interaction, with exceptions: some extroverts still enjoy some visitors. Remain attentive to what the person needs, communicating by touch if necessary and providing a relaxed, peaceful atmosphere. You may want to play some calming music or pray with the person when he is awake. Be aware that even though his eyes are closed, he may still hear you. Do not make any remarks about him while near his bed.

Sleeping more. Along with a loss of energy, the person may be sleeping more. Sometimes he or she may drop off to sleep in the middle of a conversation.

Appetite changes. The patient may express an interest in a certain food, but claim to be full after a bite or two. Again, it may take too much energy for her to eat. One doctor put it this way: "The mind is telling the body to shut down." Offer fluids or cut-up fruits. A bendable straw is helpful for drinking liquids. It can be difficult for family members to accept that their loved one has little interest in food, and they may be tempted to try to persuade him to eat. This will only create anxiety. Let the patient decide when and what he wants to eat, and offer small portions of soft food.

Difficulty swallowing. This further complicates eating and drinking. Don't try to force foods on the sick person, which may lead to choking. Offer very small portions (a spoonful) of soft foods, such as apple-sauce, mashed potatoes, or yogurt. Liquids can also be offered by spoon, if the patient is unable to use a straw. Medications may need to be broken down and mixed with soft foods. A wet washcloth may be soothing on the lips, and small ice chips can relieve a dry mouth. For dry lips, lip balm may help.

Cognitive changes, agitation, and restlessness. This may come as a surprise after a period of sleepiness. A person may have repetitive motions, such as reaching up, grasping at bedclothes, or kicking at blankets. The patient may see and talk to beings no one else can see. Some seem to talk to deceased relatives or friends. Don't try to bring them back to your reality; this is the reality they are experiencing now. Comfort the patient by being present by touch or by gentle massage. Speak calmly. You may want to try reminiscing about some pleasant memory of the past. If she becomes agitated, her doctor may prescribe medication to help her relax.

Incontinence and involuntary elimination. As the person weakens, he may lose control over bodily functions. It is truly an act of love to help someone with these issues. Pads and adult diapers are available to help with incontinence and elimination. Keep the patient clean and dry, and treat him with dignity. Help to preserve his privacy by keeping him covered. A warm sponge bath may be welcome, and some lotion that is not strongly scented may give relief from dryness.

Change in temperature. As the heart weakens, circulation is affected and body temperature can fluctuate. The skin may be ruddy and feel hot. The patient may kick off the bedclothes and a moment later, she may feel cold. Simply keep the person comfortable, adding an extra blanket if needed or covering her with a light sheet. This requires patience of the caregiver, as there might be a frequent fluctuation of temperature in the patient that requires attention.

Surprising alertness. Shortly before death, the person may wake up and be alert. He may suddenly be able to carry on a conversation and may even have an interest in food. It is as if the life force gathers one final time. This time is truly a gift to loved ones who may wish to express their love and affection at this time, while the person is alert and fully conscious. This is a time to call the family together for a final visit. The family may wish to recall some kindness or happy occasions. Unfortunately, this time does not last long and the patient soon may lapse into unconsciousness.

Change in breathing pattern. A change in the breathing pattern occurs as the patient approaches death. It becomes more labored, and the ribcage may move up and down with each breath. The exhalation of breath takes longer than the inhalation; there may be prolonged pauses between breaths, sometimes what seems like several seconds. There may be a rattling noise as the patient labors to breathe. Hearing is the last sense to leave, so speak in a calm voice and use reassuring words that bring comfort. The patient will finally stop breathing, often in a very peaceful way.

My daughter was visiting with a friend several days before her death. The friend told my daughter that she was hearing music and wondered if my daughter heard it as well. My daughter said no, that she did not, and asked her friend what it sounded like. She hummed a little, then said it sounded like angels singing. It was a great comfort to the young woman to know that someone had listened to her and believed what she said.

To be with someone as he or she dies is a powerful experience, although it can be very disconcerting. Remember to keep your focus on the patient's needs at this time, but do not forget to be very gentle with yourself as well. This is a time that brings up strong emotions that can be overwhelming, and sometimes fear can be prevalent. Ask for help from others around you when needed, including professional health care workers and caregivers.

One afternoon, some years ago, I was going out to a meeting. Suddenly, an older woman who was seriously ill came into my mind. The retirement home where she lived was on my way to the meeting, and I decided to stop by and see her.

Dorothea recognized me immediately. She smiled and I took her hand, which she lightly squeezed. I sat with her quietly for a while, holding her hand, and then I said a prayer. Her breathing had become irregular, with interspersed pauses.

It was very quiet in this section of the building, and after a while I realized that Dorothea had simply stopped breathing. She looked peaceful and serene. I felt it was a great gift to be able to share this moment with her.

After death, the body seems incomplete, altered, a shell, missing the part that enlivens us and animates us, our personality—our soul. Faith can help us accept that the one who has died is now joined with all those who were part of his or her life, those whom they have loved and who have gone before them. We believe that they are now with God in a fuller way than was possible during their life on earth.

Chapter Nine

Praying with Someone Who Is Dying

Let my prayer be counted as incense before
you,
and the lifting up of my hands as an evening
sacrifice. (Psalm 141:2)

*P*rayer has an important place when visiting a dying person; however, it should not be the only reason for the visit. People who immediately open their prayer book when entering a sickroom miss the opportunity to help the dying person in simple, human ways. When the needs of the body are unmet, real prayer does not take place. Is it not prayer as well to bring the patient a cool glass of water when thirsty? To listen to their worries and concerns, even to fluff up a pillow and comb their hair?

Always ask the patient if she would like you to pray with her. Do not assume that someone wants to pray just because you think it's a good idea. If the answer is yes, ask if the person would like to pray for something in particular; most patients do indeed have definite prayer requests. Often they wish to pray for their family or for a loved one. Some wish to say a prayer of forgiveness or of thanks.

Besides traditional prayers such as the Our Father, Hail Mary, and Glory Be, here are some prayers I have found helpful to say with someone who is dying.

In Gratitude

Dear Lord,

I come to you with a thankful heart.

I thank you for the kindness shown me

by the doctors and nurses who are caring for me.

I thank you for those who have visited me and contacted me,

for friends and family who have prayed for me,

for the ones who have cared about me,

and for the dear ones who have loved me.

Keep them all in your care

and bless them for their abundant kindness. Amen.

Prayer of Forgiveness

Heavenly Father,

I ask forgiveness of anyone I have wronged
during my lifetime.

I sincerely regret any harm I may have caused.

Likewise, I am willing to forgive anyone who has
wronged me.

When my time comes,

open your arms to me and accept me

into your heavenly kingdom, where I will be

united with all the loved ones who have gone before
me,

and I will rejoice forever in your saving presence.
Amen.

Psalm 23

The LORD is my shepherd, I shall not want.

He makes me lie down in green pastures;
he leads me beside still waters;

he restores my soul.
He leads me in right paths
for his name's sake.

Even though I walk through the darkest valley,
I fear no evil;

for you are with me;
    your rod and your staff—
    they comfort me.
You prepare a table before me
    in the presence of my enemies;
you anoint my head with oil;
    my cup overflows.
Surely goodness and mercy shall follow me
    all the days of my life,
and I shall dwell in the house of the LORD
    my whole life long.

Here are some other suggestions for passages from Scripture:

Psalm 25

Psalm 91

Psalm 121

Job 19:23–27

Matthew 25:1–13

Luke 22:39–46

Luke 23:44–49

Luke 24:1–8

John 6:37–40

John 14:1–6, 23, 27

1 John 4:16

Revelation 21:1–7

Peace Prayer of St. Francis

Lord, make me an instrument of your peace.
Where there is hatred, let me sow love;
where there is injury, pardon;
where there is doubt, faith;
where there is despair, hope;
where there is darkness, light;
and where there is sadness, joy.

O Divine Master, grant that I may not so much seek
to be consoled as to console;
to be understood as to understand;
to be loved as to love.
For it is in giving that we receive;
it is in pardoning that we are pardoned;
and it is in dying that we are born to eternal life.
Amen.

Healing

They say that time heals all wounds
but time seems to expand, stand still.
We would like to rush the process,
move swiftly through the present,
reach the goal in record time.
Yet healing takes patience;

waiting, hoping, praying.
Lord, give us the patience
to await healing in your time,
not to give up hope,
and to be thankful each new day
for the gift of life,
That you have given us. Amen.

Mary's Canticle (The Magnificat)

My soul magnifies the Lord,
and my spirit rejoices in God my Savior,
for he has looked with favor on the lowliness of his
servant.
Surely, from now on all generations will call me
blessed;
for the Mighty One has done great things for me,
and holy is his name.
His mercy is for those who fear him
from generation to generation.
He has shown strength with his arm;
he has scattered the proud in the thoughts of their
hearts.
He has brought down the powerful from their thrones,
and lifted up the lowly;

he has filled the hungry with good things,

    and sent the rich away empty.

He has helped his servant Israel,

    in remembrance of his mercy,

according to the promise he made to our ancestors,

    to Abraham and to his descendants forever.

    (Luke 1:46–55)

When Someone Is Near Death

Go forth, dear one, from this world,

in the name of the Father who created you,

the Son who redeemed you,

And the Holy Spirit who sanctified you.

rest gently in the loving arms of God,

and shine in the divine light forever. Amen.

For Those Who Mourn

Gracious God,

look down on us in our sorrow and grief.

Comfort us in our mourning;

give us certainty in our doubt;

and the courage to live through this hour.

Increase our faith, that we may come to know better

your eternal love. Amen.

Notes

1. Mary Bauer, "Importance of Human Touch,"
    Livestrong.com, January 28, 2014, http://www.
    livestrong.com/article/186495-importance-of
    -human-touch/.

2. Mother Teresa, *Come Be My Light: The Private Writings of
    the Saint of Calcutta*, ed. Brian Kolodiejchuk (New
    York: Image, 2009), pp. 186–87.

3. James Martin, S.J., "A Saint's Dark Night,"
    The New York Times, August 29, 2007. www.
    nytimes.com/2007/08/29/opinion/29martin.
    html?th&emc=th&_r=0.

4. "A Chart Review of Seven Hundred Eighty-Two
    Deaths in Hospitals, Nursing Homes, and
    Hospice/Home Care," *Journal of Palliative Medicine* 8,
    no. 4 (2005), pp. 789–796.

ABOUT THE AUTHOR

Margrit Anna Banta has spent over thirty years as a
pastoral associate working with the sick and dying in
homes, hospital, and nursing homes. She developed
and taught a course at DePaul Nursing School in
Norfolk, VA, to help nurses and other caregivers talk
to terminally ill and dying patients.